KRIEGER ©
IN THE BEGINNING...

A COLLECTION OF
CARICATURES AND POLITICAL CARTOONS
BY BOB KRIEGER

NEW STAR BOOKS
VANCOUVER

Most of the cartoons within appeared originally in the *Province*, the Vancouver *Courier* and the *Jewish Western Bulletin*. A few have never been published because editors are no fools.

Special thanks to the Honorable Dr. Patrick Lucey McGeer, formerly minister responsible for the Insurance Corporation of B.C. Had you not been such an inviting target I might have a real job.

—*Bob Krieger*

Copyright © 1981 Bob Krieger
All Rights Reserved

First printing November 1981
5 4 3 2 1

Design consultant: Gordon J. Miller

Canadian Cataloguing in Publication Data
Krieger, Bob, 1954-
    Krieger—In the beginning

    ISBN 0-919888-49-6 (bound)
    ISBN 0-919888-44-5 (pbk.)

    1. Canada—Politics and government—1963-
—Caricatures and cartoons. 2. World politics—
1975-1985—Caricatures and cartoons. 3. Canadian
wit and humor, Pictorial. I. Title. II. Title:
In the beginning.
    NC1449.K74A4 1981   741.5'971   C81-091387-9

The publisher is grateful for assistance
provided by the Canada Council.

New Star Books Ltd.
2504 York Avenue
Vancouver, B.C.   V6K 1E3

INTRODUCTION...

Political cartooning is an insidious craft.

Political cartoonists aren't like regular artists. No cartooning for cartooning's sake, abstract conceptualizing or inky Rorschachesques. They draw, but the similarity ends there.

Are they black and white realists? Hardly. They have whimsy. The plain truth would send readers running, screaming into the streets. Besides, the editors would never permit it.

Political cartoonists must tell the truth, palatably, without inducing general hysteria or mass suicide. Yet they must say what must be said. What could be more awkward or difficult in our horrific, ridiculous, arbitrary world?

So political cartoonists develop finely-tuned insidiousness.

They get to you. They make you laugh at things that are hardly funny, really. They bore holes in your defences while you sit smiling. They inject you with biting, intelligent images and then cover the holes with their ink-stained thumbs and shake you 'til you are enlightened.

In the Beginning Bob Krieger created the Klansman who looks like a rumpled adolescent just home from trick or treats. That's so you could stand to look at him. And Menachem Begin in coke-bottle glasses dialing Greenpeace. How else to swallow our teetering presence on the brink of nuclear nightmare but with a drop of seltzer?

Humanized sacred cows is Bob's black and white business. His secret is, we color it ourselves.

Gail Mainster, a friend

3

To Charlie and Kit, with inexpressible appreciation. Can I ever repay you? (Perhaps dim sum on me every day for... two days?)

CANADA...

Canada Day

China arms shoppers rebuffed by Canada

McDonald Commission releases report on
RCMP wrong-doings

9

Petrocan buys Fina oil

11

Joe survives leadership challenge

Tories push Commons debate on capital punishment

Broadbent drops in on Castro in Havana

B.C. fishermen fail to catch Romeo LeBlanc for discussion

Czech hockey stars given refugee status

Urea formaldehyde poses threat to homeowners

Native people charge Indian Affairs with partying on department funds

Courts award Musqueam Band $10 million in golf course rip-off

Oilers sweep Habs in playoffs

NEWS ITEM: PARTI QUEBECOIS MAY FIELD FEDERAL CANDIDATES.

22

THE ECONOMY...

MacEachenomics

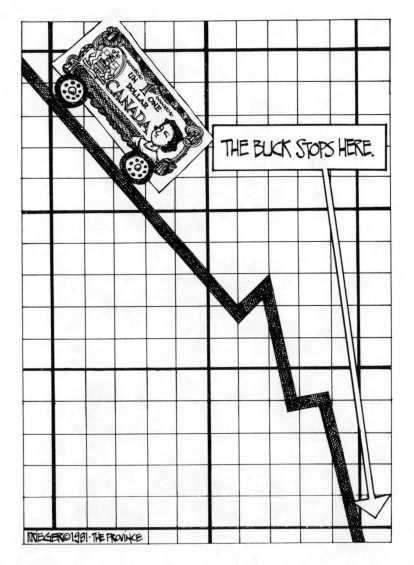

31

The housing crisis

BRITISH COLUMBIA...

FOR SALE

ELLEN MACKAY

VANDER ZALM CARTOONS

JACK KELLY

GRACIE FINGER

BCRIC

DAN CAMPBELL FIASCO $

KERSTER CAPER

ICBC

B.C. Ombudsman Karl Friedman investigates
Gracie's Finger affair

Huge profits for those who get land out of B.C.'s Agricultural Land Reserve

Socreds hire Hollywood film man to improve image

$15,000 spent on Socred TV spectacular

41

Pat McGeer, former minister responsible for B.C.'s auto insurance corporation... "Let them sell their cars"

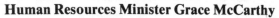

Dave Barrett

April 14

Dear Editor,
    I feel compelled to write and express my feeling that B.C.'s doctors are being unreasonable in their contract demands.
        Name withheld
        (In case I get sick)

KRIEGER © 1981
THE PROVINCE

April Fool's Day

50

HUMAN RIGHTS...

**Vancouver lawyer John McAlpine investigates
KKK activities**

Socreds introduce anti-hate legislation

Anti-abortionist assaults free choice demonstrators

VANCOUVER...

JULY...SIGH.

City council bans street posters

Mayor Harcourt tours Japan

**While hotel workers picket, demolition crew
wrecks Devonshire**

68

NEWS ITEM: STRIKING CIVIC WORKERS TO GET NEW OFFER.

72

...on the heels of the long civic strike

B.C. Tel workers picket B.C. Ferries terminal

Firemen threaten walkout

The baseball strike of 1981...

...ends

President Reagan fires air traffic controllers...

. . . and flies to California

Labour Day 1981

THE UNITED STATES...

Reverend Jerry Falwell

OUT WITH THE OLD... IN WITH THE ARCHAIC.

89

**America's best-dressed woman
wears bullet-proof underwear**

Soviets close to N-bomb production

92

U.S. admits to shooting down own plane in April drill

95

U.S. hostage rescue mission fails

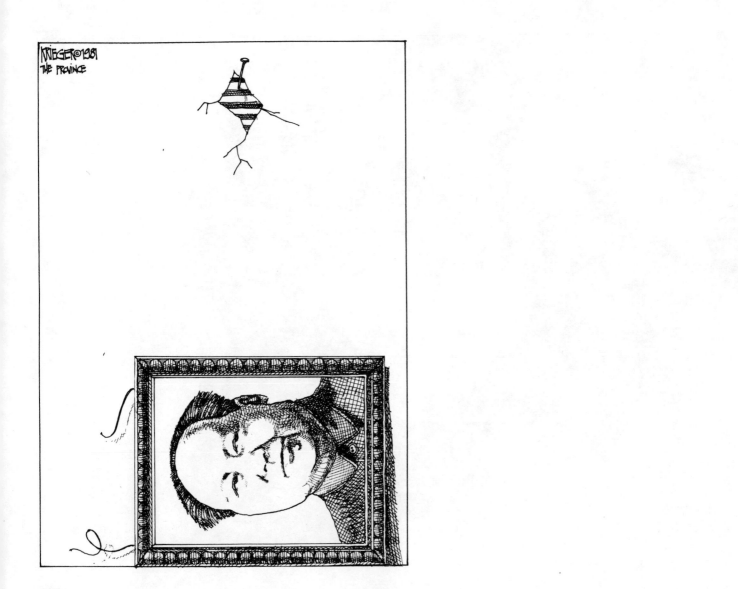

U.S. envoy Phillip Habib wins Mid-East ceasefire

UN condemns...

...Israeli raid on Iraqi nuclear reactor

Begin forms minority government

Vatican's books show deficit

MI5 head a double agent

The Iron Maiden

Charlie and Princess Di

THE ECOLOGY...

112

Big game hunters stalk Greenpeacers

Californians oppose malathion spray

Fundamentalists want creation theory taught in science classes

Exploding pop bottles ordered off shelves

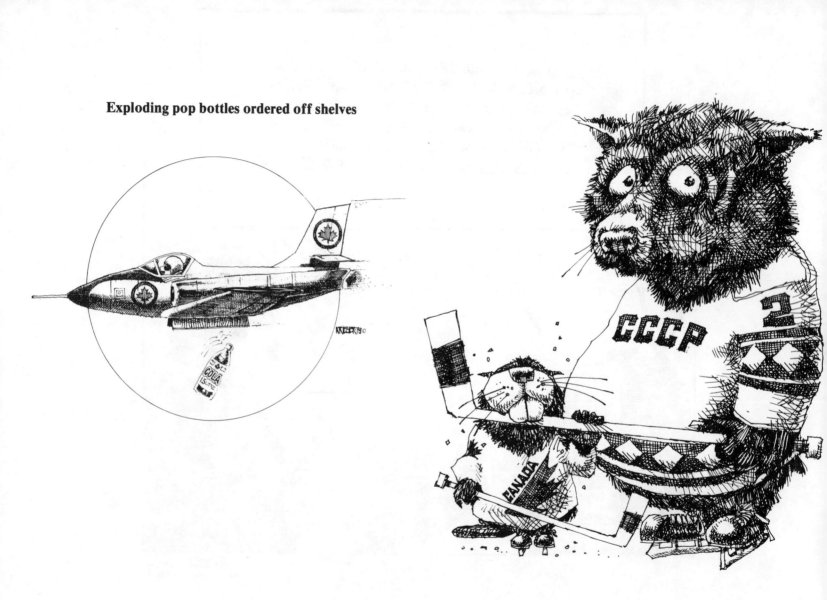

Kent commission investigates newspaper competition